A COMPREHENSIVE VALENCIA TRAVEL GUIDE 2024

The beauty of Valencia

All you need to know before traveling to Valencia in 2024

MASON WEST

Copyright ©2023 by mason west

all rights reserved. no part of this publication may be reproduced, distributed or transmitted in any form or by any means, including photocopying, recording ot other electronic or mechanical methods without the prior written permission of the publisher, except in the case of brief quotations embodied in critical reviews and certain other noncommercial uses permitted by copyright law.

CONTENTS

INTRODUCTION..6
   But why Valencia, you ask?..7
CHAPTER 1: FAST FACTS..9
   Essential information about Valencia...............................9
CHAPTER 2: PLANNING YOUR TRIP.....................13
   When to Visit...13
   Visa requirements..16
CHAPTER 3: GETTING THERE..............................20
    flights..20
    Trains..22
    BUSES..25
    Getting Around..26
    Where to Stay..29
    Apartments..32
    Unique stays..35
    Budget-friendly options...38
    Packing Essentials..40
    Activities:...42
CHAPTER 4: EXPERIENCING VALENCIA..............44
   Top Attractions to visit in Valencia.................................44
   Cultural Immersion..51
   Festival Delights:...52
   Local Immersions:...52
   Beyond the City...56
   Activities for Everyone...59
   Hidden Gems..63
CHAPTER 5: SAVOURING VALENCIA....................68
   Traditional Dishes..68
   Must-Try Local Specialties:...69

Unveiling culinary gems.. 69
Food Tours and Markets...................................... 72
Wine and Drinks... 74

CHAPTER 6: PRACTICAL INFORMATION.............. 79
Currency Exchange:.. 79
Budgeting Tips:..80
Accepted Payment Methods:..80
Communication.. 81
Phone Cards.. 82
Basic Spanish Phrases... 82
Safety and Security.. 84
Emergency Numbers.. 85
Scams to Avoid..85
Sustainable Travel... 86

CHAPTER 7: FINDING THE BEST TRAVEL DEALS ... 89
Finding Affordable Flights..89
Finding Affordable Accommodation:...........................90
Finding Affordable Activities:....................................... 90
Budgeting Strategies... 92
Free and Cheap Activities... 94
Eating Like a Local...98
Transportation Tips..101

CHAPTER 8: ITINERARY.. 104
3 Days.. 104
7 days Itinerary...107
2 Weeks Itinerary... 111

CONCLUSION.. 114

INTRODUCTION

Valencia beckons like a sangria-soaked dream, ready to tantalize your taste buds and ignite your senses. Forget the tourist traps, this vibrant city on Spain's sunny coast is where laid-back charm meets electrifying energy, ancient history whispers secrets in its cobbled streets, and futuristic architecture soars towards the azure sky.

Valencia isn't just another pretty face (though let's be honest, it's drop-dead gorgeous). It's a city that pulsates with life, a kaleidoscope of cultures, where tapas crawl at sunset turns into beach bonfires under a star-studded sky. Think: sun-drenched days spent strolling along the golden sands, followed by nights filled with laughter in hidden plazas and fiery flamenco performances.

But why Valencia, you ask?

Buckle up, amigos, because here's why this city should be your next adventure:

1. Foodie Paradise: Forget boring buffets, Valencia is a gourmet playground. Fresh seafood straight from the Med, melt-in-your-mouth paella, and tapas that are tiny flavor bombs – your taste buds will do a happy dance.

2. Beach Bum Bliss: Picture this: turquoise waters lapping at soft sand, beach bars serving up icy cocktails, and sunshine warming your skin. Valencia's beaches are pure bliss, perfect for lazy days soaking up the rays or trying your hand at water sports.

3. History Buff Heaven: From the majestic Silk Exchange to the awe-inspiring Cathedral, Valencia's history is a treasure trove waiting to be explored. Wander ancient Roman ruins, get lost in medieval alleyways, and feel the weight of time in every cobblestone.

4. Art Attack!: Forget dusty museums, Valencia's art scene is as vibrant as its street murals. From the futuristic City of Arts and Sciences to hidden galleries showcasing local talent, prepare to be dazzled by artistic expression in all its forms.

5. Fiesta Forever: Valencia knows how to throw a party! From the world-famous Las Fallas festival with its towering, combustible sculptures, to lively street parties and buzzing bars, get ready to shake your groove thing and embrace the fiesta spirit.

This is just a taste of what Valencia has in store. So, ditch the ordinary, pack your sense of adventure, and get ready to fall head over heels for this sun-kissed Spanish gem. Your unforgettable adventure awaits!

P.S. We haven't even mentioned the hidden gems, the quirky traditions, and the friendly locals who will make you feel like family. Stay tuned for more insider tips and tricks to make your Valencia trip unforgettable!

CHAPTER 1: FAST FACTS

Essential information about Valencia

So you've decided to ditch the ordinary and embrace the Valencian adventure! But before you jet set off, let's get you prepped with some essential info to ensure your trip is smooth sailing (or should we say, smooth sailing on the Mediterranean!).

Lingo lowdown:
• **Language:** Spanish is the official language, but don't fret if your "Hola!" is a little rusty. Many locals understand English, especially in tourist areas. Bonus points for trying a few basic Spanish phrases – it'll go a long way with the friendly Valencians!
• **Currency:** Euros are your golden ticket here. ATMs are widely available, but it's always handy to have some cash on hand for smaller purchases.

Time warp

• **Time zone:** Central European Time (CET), which is one hour ahead of Greenwich Mean Time (GMT) and six hours ahead of Pacific Standard Time (PST). Don't forget to adjust your watch – those siestas won't wait!

• **Emergency number:** 112 (for fire, ambulance, and police)

Tourist information: +34 963 92 03 00

Tech talk:

• **Power outlets:** Europe uses two-pronged plugs (Type C), so pack a universal adapter if you're coming from North America.

• **Wi-Fi:** Most hotels, restaurants, and cafes offer free Wi-Fi, so you can stay connected and share your Valencian adventures with the world (or at least your jealous friends back home).

Bonus tip: Siesta time is sacred! (This afternoon break is traditionally used for napping, relaxing, or enjoying a leisurely meal. Don't be confused if things seem a little quieter during this time – it's just the Valencian way of life! While you can certainly take a nap yourself (power naps are amazing!), you can also use this time to:

- **Explore quieter corners of the city:** Many museums and attractions have reduced hours during siesta, but this can be a great opportunity to visit off-the-beaten-path spots without the crowds.
- **Indulge in a long lunch:** Siesta is the perfect time to savor a delicious paella or tapas crawl at a leisurely pace. Many restaurants offer special siesta menus with discounted prices.
- **Seek shade and recharge:** If napping isn't your thing, find a park or shady plaza to relax, read a book, or simply people-watch. Remember, siesta isn't just about napping, it's about taking a break and slowing down the pace) Many shops and businesses close between 2pm and 5pm, so plan your sightseeing and shopping accordingly. Embrace the relaxed pace and siesta like a true Valencian.

CHAPTER 2: PLANNING YOUR TRIP

When to Visit

Choosing the ideal time to visit Valencia depends on your travel desires. Are you a beach bum craving sunshine, a history buff chasing cultural events, or a budget-conscious traveler seeking deals? Fear not, this guide will help you find the season that perfectly matches your travel goals:

Spring (March-May)

- **Weather:** Pleasant temperatures (16-23°C), ideal for sightseeing and outdoor activities.
- **Crowds:** Moderate, with an increase during Las Fallas festival (mid-March).
- **Events:** Las Fallas (spectacular fire festival), Holy Week processions, Valencia Marathon.
- **Pros:** Comfortable weather, blooming orange trees, fewer crowds than summer.
- **Cons:** Las Fallas can be expensive and crowded, some rain possible.

Summer (June-August)
- **Weather:** Hot and sunny (25-32°C), perfect for beach days and soaking up the sun.
- **Crowds**: High, especially in July and August.
- **Events:** La Tomatina tomato fight (late August), Nit de Foc fireworks festival, various music festivals.
- **Pros:** Warmest weather, vibrant nightlife, abundance of water activities.
- **Cons:** Very busy and expensive, potentially stifling heat, some shops and businesses close during siesta.

Autumn (September-November)
- **Weather:** Mellow temperatures (20-27°C), ideal for outdoor explorations.
- **Crowds:** Lower than summer, but still significant during Fallas (early September).
- **Events:** Fallas festival (early September), Rice Festival, Valencia Film Festival.
- **Pros:** Comfortable temperatures, fewer crowds, cheaper prices compared to summer.
- **Cons:** Fallas can still be crowded, some rainy days possible.

Winter (December-February)
- **Weather:** Mild temperatures (10-18°C), with occasional rain.

- **Crowds:** Lowest of the year.
- **Events:** Three Kings Parade (Epiphany), Ruzafa Carnival, Chinese New Year celebrations.
- **Pros:** Budget-friendly prices, fewer crowds, chance to experience local traditions.
- **Cons:** Cooler weather, shorter daylight hours, some attractions may have limited hours.

Bonus tip: Consider combining seasons! Valencia enjoys a long period of pleasant weather, so you could opt for a shoulder season trip (spring or fall) to enjoy comfortable temperatures, moderate crowds, and a mix of events.

Ultimately, the best time to visit Valencia is the time that best suits your interests and preferences. Do you crave sunshine and beach time? Go for summer! Are you a history buff drawn to cultural events? Spring or fall might be perfect. Remember, there's no one-size-fits-all answer, so choose the season that makes your Valencian adventure dreams come true!

Visa requirements

Before you book your flights and pack your sunscreen, let's navigate the sometimes-confusing world of visa requirements for your Valencian adventure. Don't worry, sunshine seeker, this guide will help you determine if you need a visa and, if so, how to acquire it painlessly.

First things first, nationality matters, your visa requirements depend on your nationality. Check the official Spanish Ministry of Foreign Affairs website or your local Spanish embassy/consulate to see if you need a visa for traveling to Spain.

Good news for most travelers
- **Schengen Visa Holders:** If you hold a valid Schengen visa issued by any Schengen member state, you're good to go! You can stay in Spain for up to 90 days within a 180-day period without needing a separate Spanish visa.
- **Visa-free countries:** Citizens of many countries, including most of Europe, the US, Canada, Australia, and New Zealand, don't require a visa for short tourist stays in Spain. Check the official list on the Spanish Ministry of Foreign Affairs website for specifics.

Not so lucky? Don't fret:
- **National Visas:** If you need a visa to stay in Spain for longer than 90 days or for reasons other than tourism (e.g., work, study), you'll need a

national visa. These require more paperwork and processing time, so plan accordingly.
- **Where to apply:** Contact the Spanish embassy or consulate in your home country for detailed information on applying for a national visa.

Costs to consider:
- **Schengen Visa Fee:** €80 for adults, free for children under 6.
- **National Visa Fee:** Varies depending on the visa type and purpose. Expect a range of €60-€90, but check with your embassy/consulate for exact fees.
- **Additional fees:** Processing fees, courier charges, and passport photos may apply.

Visa Documents:
The specific documents required for your visa application will vary depending on your nationality and visa type. However, some general documents you'll likely need include:
- Completed visa application form
- Valid passport with at least three blank pages and remaining validity beyond your intended stay in Spain
- Two recent passport-sized photos
- Proof of travel insurance
- Proof of sufficient financial means to support your stay (e.g., bank statements, employment letter)

- Flight itinerary and accommodation booking confirmation
- For national visas: Additional documents may be required depending on the visa type. Check with your embassy/consulate for details.

Bonus Tip: Apply for your visa well in advance of your trip, especially during peak season (typically June to August). Processing times can vary, so give yourself ample buffer to avoid last-minute scrambles.

Remember, even if you don't need a visa, ensure your passport is valid for at least three months beyond your intended stay in Spain. With some planning and preparation, visa requirements won't stand in the way of your Valencian adventure! Now, onto the exciting world of finding your perfect accommodation

CHAPTER 3: GETTING THERE

flights

Ready to trade your land legs for wings and embark on your Valencian adventure? Let's explore the exciting world of flights to get you there in no time!

Direct Flights:

- **Convenience king:** If speed and ease are your top priorities, direct flights are your golden ticket. Expect travel times between 1-3 hours depending on your origin city.

- **Cost considerations:** Prices can vary greatly, so compare different airlines and book in advance, especially during peak season (June-August). Budget airlines like Ryanair and Vueling may offer competitive fares starting around €50-€100 for short-haul flights within Europe, but check baggage fees and additional costs. Major airlines like Iberia, British Airways, and KLM offer more comfort and amenities with prices typically starting around €150-€250 for short-haul flights and increasing for long-haul journeys.

- **Major airlines:** Iberia, British Airways, KLM, Lufthansa, Air France, TAP Portugal, SWISS

Connecting Flights:
- **Budget-friendly option:** If direct flights are out of your budget or not available from your location, consider connecting flights with a stopover in another European city. This can be a great way to break up the journey and explore another destination on your way.
- **Travel time trade-off:** Expect longer travel times compared to direct flights, potentially ranging from 4-8 hours or even more depending on your stopover duration.
- **Airline combinations:** Explore various airlines and routes to find the best combination of price and travel time. Consider budget airlines like Ryanair, Vueling, EasyJet for the first leg and major airlines for the connecting flight for a balance of cost and comfort. Budget airlines can offer flights within Europe for as low as €20-€40, but connecting flights can add complexity and potential delays.

Estimated Costs:
- **Direct Flights:** As mentioned above, prices can vary greatly depending on various factors. Expect a range of €50-€250+ for short-haul flights within Europe and even higher for long-haul journeys. Be

sure to compare airlines, book in advance, and factor in baggage fees and other hidden costs.
- **Connecting Flights:** Can be cheaper than direct flights, especially if you combine budget airlines for different legs. However, factor in additional costs like baggage fees for each flight and potential airport transfers between terminals. Budget airlines like Ryanair and EasyJet can offer connecting flights within Europe for as low as €30-€50 per leg, but remember to add baggage fees and connection costs.

Bonus Tip: Consider flying into a nearby airport like Alicante (ALC) or Barcelona (BCN) and taking a connecting train or bus to Valencia for potentially cheaper options, especially if you're flexible with your travel dates and times.

Trains

Dreaming of picturesque landscapes and comfortable travel? Choo-choo aboard the adventure as we explore trains as your gateway to Valencia!

High-Speed Bliss:
- **Speed demon:** AVE trains, operated by Renfe, zoom you to Valencia at impressive speeds, whisking you away in just 1h 45m from Madrid and

3h 05m from Barcelona. Perfect for time-conscious travelers or those who want to maximize their time in Valencia.

- **Comfort king:** Settle into spacious seats, enjoy ample legroom, and relish onboard amenities like Wi-Fi, charging points, and a cafe-bar.

- **Cost considerations:** Expect tickets to start around €40-€60 for short journeys and increase for longer distances. Book in advance, especially during peak season, to score the best deals.

Regional Charm:

- **Leisurely explorer:** Hop on regional Renfe trains for a more leisurely journey, soaking in the Spanish countryside along the way. Travel times are longer (e.g., 4-7 hours from Madrid), but the scenic routes offer a unique travel experience.

- **Budget-friendly option:** Regional trains are typically cheaper than AVEs, with tickets starting around €20-€30 for shorter journeys. Ideal for budget-conscious travelers who enjoy slower travel.

- **Limited frequency:** Be aware that regional trains have fewer daily departures compared to AVEs, so plan your trip accordingly.

Night Trains:

- **Sleep and save:** Catch some zzz's while traveling overnight on Trenhotel, Renfe's night train service.

Arrive in Valencia refreshed and ready to explore!
- **Cost-effective choice:** Night trains can be a budget-friendly option, especially if you factor in the cost of hotel accommodation for one night.
- **Limited routes:** Currently, Trenhotel only offers one overnight route from Madrid to Valencia.

Bonus Tip: Combine train travel with other options! For example, fly into Barcelona and take a scenic AVE train to Valencia, or take a regional train from a nearby city like Zaragoza for a slower, more immersive experience.

BUSES

Ready to hit the open road and experience the Spanish landscape on a budget? Buckle up, budget traveler, because buses are your ticket to a cost-effective and scenic journey to Valencia!

Long-Distance Comfort:
- **Budget champion:** Bus travel is the most affordable way to reach Valencia, with tickets starting as low as €15-€20 for short journeys and increasing for longer distances. Ideal for budget-conscious travelers who don't mind slower travel times.

- **Comfort considerations:** While not as luxurious as trains, modern long-distance buses offer reclining seats, air conditioning, Wi-Fi (sometimes), and onboard toilets for a comfortable journey.
- **Travel Time Trade-off:** Expect longer travel times compared to trains, ranging from 4-8 hours or even more depending on your origin city and route. Pack some entertainment and snacks for the ride!

Popular Bus Companies:
- **Alसा:** Spain's largest bus company, offering extensive coverage and comfortable coaches.
- **FlixBus:** A budget-friendly option with a large network across Europe, known for its competitive prices.
- **Eurolines:** Another budget-friendly option with international routes connecting Valencia to other European cities.

Additional Considerations:
- **Luggage fees:** Check the baggage allowance and potential fees before booking.
- **Rest stops:** Factor in rest stop breaks, which can add to the overall travel time.

- **Night buses:** Consider overnight buses to save on accommodation costs, but be prepared for limited legroom and sleep interruptions.

Bonus Tip: Combine bus travel with other options! For example, fly into a major city like Barcelona and take a budget-friendly bus to Valencia, or take a regional train from a closer location for a more scenic experience.

Getting Around

Valencia's vibrant energy isn't confined to its stunning architecture and delicious cuisine; it extends to its diverse and convenient transportation options. Whether you're an eco-conscious cyclist, a time-pressed sightseer, or a budget-savvy explorer, Valencia has a mode of transport to match your needs and preferences. Let's delve into each option to help you navigate the city like a seasoned local:

Public Transportation:
- **Metro:** Valencia's metro network is the fastest and most efficient way to travel around the city, reaching most major attractions and neighborhoods. With 9 lines and over 100 stations, the metro is clean, reliable, and affordable (single tickets start around €1.50). Download the official

Metrovalencia app for route planning, real-time updates, and ticket purchases.
- **Tram:** Trams complement the metro network, offering scenic rides through historic areas and along the beach. Three tram lines connect key locations like the City of Arts and Sciences, the marina, and the Cabanyal neighborhood. Tickets are integrated with the metro system, so you can use the same ticket for both.
- **Bus:** Valencia's extensive bus network covers areas not served by the metro or tram, providing access to suburbs and outlying districts. Buses are generally slower than the metro but offer a wider reach for €1.50 per trip. Be sure to validate your ticket upon boarding.

Green Getaways:
- **Bike Rentals:** Valencia is a cyclist's paradise with flat terrain, dedicated bike lanes, and a well-developed bike rental system, Valenbisi. Rent a bike for a few hours or longer and explore the city at your own pace. Day passes start around €5, and weekly subscriptions offer even better value.
- **Walking:** Valencia's compact city center is best explored on foot. Stroll along the Turia Gardens, meander through the charming El Carmen neighborhood, or wander the lively Mercado

Central, soaking in the sights, sounds, and aromas. Comfortable walking shoes are a must!

Taxis and Rideshares:
- Taxis: While not the most budget-friendly option, taxis offer convenience, especially for late-night journeys or carrying luggage. Metered fares apply, and you can hail taxis on the street or pre-book through apps.

- Rideshares: Ridesharing services like Uber and Cabify operate in Valencia, offering competitive fares and app-based booking. Consider this option for point-to-point travel, especially if you're familiar with using these services.

Additional Tips:
- Valencia Tourist Card: Consider purchasing a Valencia Tourist Card for unlimited travel on public transport, including metro, tram, and bus, for 24, 48, or 72 hours. This can be a cost-effective option if you plan to use public transport extensively.

- BONO Transporte: If you're staying for an extended period, consider purchasing a BONO Transporte, a rechargeable travel card offering discounted fares on public transport.

- Safety: All modes of transport in Valencia are safe and reliable. However, be mindful of your belongings, especially in crowded areas.

Where to Stay

Valencia's vibrant spirit isn't just reflected in its attractions, but also in its diverse accommodation options. Whether you're a luxury seeker, a history buff, or a budget-conscious explorer, the city offers a haven to suit your needs and dreams. So, unpack your bags and step into the world of Valencian hospitality!

Luxury Lodgings:
- **The Westin Valencia (from €400 per night):** Immerse yourself in opulent comfort at this 5-star haven, boasting panoramic city views, a Michelin-starred restaurant, and a rooftop infinity pool. Perfect for those who crave indulgence and unparalleled service.
- **Hospes Palau de la Mar (from €300 per night):** Dive into Valencia's rich history at this 19th-century palace-turned-hotel. Luxuriate in its opulent décor, serene spa, and gourmet dining, all footsteps away from the iconic Turia Gardens.

Mid-Range Marvels:
- **Caro Hotel (from €200 per night):** Embrace Valencian charm at this stylish boutique hotel nestled in the heart of the El Carmen neighborhood.

Enjoy its rooftop terrace with city views, cozy rooms, and friendly atmosphere.

- **Hotel Neptuno (from €150 per night):** Savor the sea breeze and stunning beach views at this modern hotel steps away from the Malvarrosa beachfront. Unwind in its rooftop pool, indulge in delicious tapas, and explore the vibrant maritime atmosphere.

Budget-Friendly Gems:
- **Hotel Kramer (from €50 per night):** This family-run hotel is situated in the historic El Carmen neighborhood, offering a charming and central location close to the Mercado Central and Plaza de la Reina. Guests praise its clean and comfortable rooms, friendly staff, and delicious breakfast.
- **Petit Palace Plaza de la Reina (from €70 per night):** Nestled in the heart of the Old Town, this charming hotel boasts stunning views of the Plaza de la Reina and is steps away from the Valencia Cathedral and Central Market. Guests appreciate its bright and airy rooms, central location, and easy access to public transportation.
- **Casual Vintage Valencia (from €45 per night):** This trendy hostel is located in the lively Ruzafa district, known for its vibrant nightlife and art scene. It offers dorm beds and private rooms at

affordable prices, along with a rooftop terrace, bar, and social atmosphere.

- **The River Hostel (from €35 per night):** This popular hostel is situated in the Ciutat Vella district, close to the Turia Gardens and Colón metro station. It offers a mix of dorm beds and private rooms, along with a communal kitchen, bar, and rooftop terrace with city views.

- **Hostal El Cid (from €30 per night):** This traditional hostel is located in the El Carmen neighborhood, offering a budget-friendly option close to major attractions like the Torres de Quart and Lonja de la Seda. Guests appreciate its friendly atmosphere, helpful staff, and shared kitchen facilities.

Remember:

- **Seasonality:** Prices fluctuate depending on the season, with peak season (June-August) seeing the highest rates. Book in advance to secure the best deals, especially for popular hotels.

- **Location:** Consider your priorities – proximity to attractions, nightlife, or the beach – when choosing your accommodation.

- **Amenities:** Decide which amenities are important to you, such as breakfast, a pool, or a spa, and filter your search accordingly.

Apartments

Embrace the freedom and flexibility of apartment living in Valencia, a fantastic alternative to hotels for budget-minded travelers or those seeking a home away from home. Whether you're exploring solo, with family, or in a group, an apartment offers a comfortable base to explore the city at your own pace, complete with kitchen facilities and local character.

Charming Neighborhood Gems
- **El Carmen:** Dive into Valencia's historic heart, brimming with narrow streets, charming squares, and vibrant nightlife. Find apartments here close to major attractions like the Torres de Quart and Lonja de la Seda. Expect prices to range from €50-€100 per night for a studio, increasing for larger apartments.
- **Ruzafa:** Discover the trendy and artistic side of Valencia in this up-and-coming district. Modern apartments here are close to lively bars, cafes, and unique shops. Prices typically start around €60-€80 per night for a studio.
- **Ciudad Vella:** Experience the city's ancient roots in this historic district, home to the Valencia Cathedral and Central Market. Apartments here

offer a central location steeped in history, with prices ranging from €70-€90 per night for a studio.
- **Cabanyal:** Savor the seaside atmosphere in this traditional fisherman's neighborhood. Find apartments here with stunning beach views and a relaxed vibe, perfect for enjoying the Mediterranean lifestyle. Expect prices to start around €80-€100 per night for a studio.

Finding Your Perfect Fit
- **Airbnb:** Explore a diverse range of apartments in various neighborhoods, budgets, and styles. From cozy studios to spacious lofts, you're sure to find something that suits your needs.
- **Booking.com:** Discover a curated selection of apartments, often with professional management and convenient cancellation policies.
- Local agencies: Consider searching for local Valencian agencies specializing in apartment rentals. They often offer unique properties and personalized service.

Cost Considerations
- **Seasonality:** Remember, prices fluctuate with the seasons. Expect higher rates during peak season (June-August) and book well in advance for popular neighborhoods.

- **Size and location:** Larger apartments and those in central locations will naturally cost more. Determine your priorities and budget accordingly.
- **Amenities:** Consider factors like Wi-Fi, air conditioning, and laundry facilities when comparing prices.

Bonus Tip: Look for apartments with balconies or terraces to enjoy the Valencian sunshine outdoors.

Remember
- **Read reviews:** Carefully read reviews from previous guests to get an idea of the apartment's cleanliness, amenities, and overall experience.
- **Communicate with the host:** Ask questions and clarify any doubts before booking. Don't hesitate to negotiate if needed.
- **Local regulations:** Be aware of any local regulations regarding short-term rentals, especially in historic districts.

Unique stays.

Valencia's vibrant spirit extends beyond conventional hotels and apartments, offering a plethora of unique stays that will transform your trip into an unforgettable adventure. From historic palaces to charming cottages, rustic farmhouses to quirky glamping experiences, prepare to be surprised and delighted by these one-of-a-kind accommodations:

1. Palacio de Santa Clara, Autograph Collection: Immerse yourself in opulent grandeur at this 15th-century palace-turned-hotel. Luxuriate in its frescoes, courtyards, and Michelin-starred restaurant, all footsteps away from the Turia Gardens. (Prices start around €350 per night)
2. Hospes Palau de la Mar: Dive into Valencia's rich history at this 19th-century palace-turned-hotel. Savor its opulent décor, serene spa, and gourmet dining, steps away from the iconic Turia Gardens. (Prices start around €300 per night)

Embrace the Rustic Charm:
3. Masia La Noguera: Escape the city buzz and reconnect with nature at this charming farmhouse nestled in the Valencian countryside. Enjoy delicious homemade meals, outdoor activities, and stunning mountain views. (Prices start around €120 per night)
4. Mas de Alzedo Eco-Resort: Immerse yourself in sustainable living at this eco-friendly resort surrounded by orange groves. Relax in cozy cabins, enjoy organic meals, and explore the surrounding nature trails. (Prices start around €150 per night)

Unique and Quirky:

5. The River Hostel: This converted 19th-century textile factory offers a vibrant atmosphere, rooftop terrace with city views, and themed dorms like "Alice in Wonderland" and "The Jungle." (Prices start around €35 per night)

6. The Dreamer Valencia: Sleep under the stars in a luxurious glamping tent equipped with a private bathroom and terrace. Enjoy the unique experience of glamping in an urban setting, close to the beach and city center. (Prices start around €100 per night)

7. Bubble Hotel: Experience a truly unique stay in a transparent bubble tent surrounded by nature, offering panoramic views of the stars and surrounding countryside. (Prices start around €180 per night)

Budget-friendly options

Escape the ordinary and experience Valencia's charm without breaking the bank! Dive into a selection of unique, budget-friendly stays that will inject personality and adventure into your trip:

History Buffs on a Shoestring:
1. Hostal Casa Almudin: Nestled in the heart of the El Carmen neighborhood, this historic hostel

boasts charming medieval walls and a friendly atmosphere. Dorms and private rooms are available, offering a comfortable and affordable base to explore the city's historic treasures. (Prices start around €25 per night for a dorm bed)

2. The Valencian Youth Hostel: Located steps away from the Valencia Cathedral, this hostel offers a blend of history and modern amenities. Explore the city's ancient roots while enjoying comfortable dorms, social spaces, and a rooftop terrace with stunning views. (Prices start around €20 per night for a dorm bed)

Nature Lovers' Delight:

3. Camping Valencia: Pitch your tent or rent a bungalow amidst the lush greenery of this campsite, just outside the city center. Enjoy the fresh air, swimming pool, and proximity to the beach for a budget-friendly and nature-filled experience. (Prices start around €20 per night for a tent pitch)

4. Valencia Camper Park: Nestled near the Albufera Natural Park, this camper park offers a peaceful setting with basic amenities for your van or motorhome. Wake up to stunning views, explore the nearby nature trails, and enjoy a truly unique Valencian experience. (Prices start around €25 per night for a camper van pitch)

Quirky and Budget-Conscious:

5. The River Hostel "Alice in Wonderland" Dorm: Indulge your inner child in this themed dorm room at The River Hostel. Bunk beds shaped like playing cards, a giant teacup, and whimsical decor create a truly unique and affordable stay. (Prices start around €35 per night for a dorm bed)

6. Purple Nest Hostel: Embrace the vibrant atmosphere of this hostel with its rooftop terrace, bar, and social events. Enjoy comfortable dorms and private rooms, all within walking distance of major attractions and nightlife. (Prices start around €20 per night for a dorm bed)

Bonus Tip: Consider house-sitting or pet-sitting through platforms like TrustedHousesitters or Rover. This can offer a free or low-cost stay while caring for someone's home and pets.

Remember

- **Book in advance:** Budget-friendly stays often have limited availability, so book well in advance, especially during peak season.
- **Consider your priorities:** Choose an option that aligns with your interests, whether it's history, nature, a social atmosphere, or a unique experience.

- **Read reviews:** Research the specific stay and read reviews from previous guests to ensure it meets your expectations.

With this guide and a little imagination, you're sure to find the perfect budget-friendly stay to add an unforgettable touch to your Valencian adventure.

Packing Essentials

Valencia's Mediterranean climate and diverse activities demand a smart packing strategy. To ensure your suitcase holds everything you need for an enjoyable trip, let's tailor your packing list based on the season and your planned activities:

Seasonality:
• **Spring (March-May):** Pack light layers like sweaters and jackets for cooler mornings and evenings, but don't forget comfortable clothes for warmer days. Include comfortable shoes for exploring and sandals for the beach.
• **Summer (June-August):** Pack light, breathable clothing like cotton t-shirts, shorts, and sundresses. Pack a hat and sunglasses for sun protection, and swimwear for enjoying the beaches and pools. Don't forget an umbrella for occasional summer showers.

- **Autumn (September-November):** Pack layers like long-sleeved shirts, light sweaters, and jeans. Comfortable walking shoes are essential as the weather becomes cooler. Consider an umbrella for potential rain.
- **Winter (December-February):** Pack warmer clothes like sweaters, jackets, and scarves for cooler temperatures. Comfortable walking shoes are still important, and consider bringing an umbrella for potential rain.

Activities:

- **Beach Bumming:** Pack plenty of swimwear, sunscreen, a hat, sunglasses, a beach towel, and a cover-up. Consider water shoes for rocky beaches.
- **Sightseeing:** Pack comfortable walking shoes, a water bottle, and a hat for exploring the city's vibrant streets. Light layers are handy for transitioning between air-conditioned museums and outdoor spaces.
- **Hiking and Outdoor Activities:** Pack appropriate footwear like hiking boots or sturdy sneakers, comfortable clothing suitable for the planned activity, sunscreen, insect repellent, and a hat.
- **Festivals and Events:** Research the specific dress code for any festivals or events you plan to

attend. Pack accordingly, considering if it's formal, casual, or costume-themed.

General Essentials

- **Comfortable walking shoes:** You'll be doing a lot of exploring, so pack shoes that are both comfortable and stylish.
- **Refillable water bottle:** Stay hydrated throughout your trip by carrying a reusable water bottle.
- **Universal adapter:** If you're traveling from abroad, pack a universal adapter to ensure your electronics stay charged.
- **Sunscreen and sunglasses:** Protect yourself from the Mediterranean sun with SPF sunscreen and sunglasses.
- **First-aid kit:** Pack basic essentials for minor cuts, scrapes, or ailments.
- **Medications:** Bring any prescription medications you need, along with over-the-counter medications like pain relievers or allergy relief.

Bonus Tip: Pack a light scarf or sarong – it's a versatile accessory that can be used as a beach cover-up, a warm layer, or even a picnic blanket.

Remember, this is just a starting point. Tailor your packing list to your specific needs, preferences, and planned activities. With careful planning and this guide, you'll be ready to pack light and explore Valencia in style and comfort!

CHAPTER 4: EXPERIENCING VALENCIA

Top Attractions to visit in Valencia

Forget the sun loungers and sangria stereotypes, Valencia is a vibrant chameleon, transforming from ancient history buff to futuristic science geek, all within a single day. Imagine strolling through sun-drenched plazas, marveling at architectural masterpieces that look like they belong on another planet, and indulging in tapas so delicious they'll make your taste buds do a flamenco dance. Buckle up, adventurer, because we're about to unlock Valencia's hidden gems and must-see marvels:

For the Time Traveler:
• **Valencia Cathedral:** This Gothic giant has been guarding the city since the 13th century. Climb the Miguelete bell tower (2€ entry) for panoramic views that stretch all the way to the sea. Feeling brave? Gargoyles with mischievous grins will keep you company on your ascent.

• **La Lonja de la Seda (The Silk Exchange):** Imagine merchants from all corners of the globe bartering for precious silks in this UNESCO World Heritage Site. The intricate carvings and grand halls (free entry!) will transport you back to Valencia's golden age of trade.

• **Valencia History Museum:** This museum is your time machine ticket, whisking you through Roman ruins, medieval battles, and the city's vibrant modern life (2€ entry). Interactive exhibits and fascinating artifacts make history come alive.

For the Future Freak:

• **Ciudad de las Artes y las Ciencias (City of Arts and Sciences):** This futuristic complex is like stepping onto the set of a sci-fi movie. Explore the Hemisfèric, a giant eye-shaped IMAX cinema (9€ entry), or get lost in the interactive exhibits of the Science Museum (8€ entry). Don't miss the stunning nighttime illuminations that transform the buildings into glowing giants.

• **L'Oceanogràfic:** Dive into the world's oceans without getting wet at this incredible aquarium (31€ entry). From playful penguins to majestic sharks, over 45,000 marine creatures await you in underwater tunnels and dazzling exhibitions.

• **Planetario:** Blast off into the cosmos at this planetarium (8€ entry), where star shows and immersive experiences will make you feel like you're floating amongst the galaxies.

For the Nature Lover:
- **Turia Gardens:** This nine-kilometer urban oasis was once a riverbed, now transformed into a haven for relaxation and recreation. Cycle along the paths, have a picnic under the palm trees, or simply soak up the sunshine (free entry!).
- **Albufera Natural Park:** Escape the city and breathe in the fresh air at this unique ecosystem (8€ entry with boat tour). Hike through rice paddies, spot diverse birdlife in the lagoons, and soak up the tranquility of this protected area.
- **Malvarrosa Beach:** Feel the soft sand between your toes and the Mediterranean breeze in your hair on Valencia's main beach. Take a dip in the crystal-clear waters (free!), build sandcastles with the kids, or simply relax with a good book and the sound of waves crashing.

For the Foodie:
- **Central Market:** This bustling market is a feast for the senses, overflowing with fresh produce, local delicacies, and handcrafted goodies. Sample seasonal fruits and cured meats, grab a delicious "bocadillo" (sandwich) for a picnic, or simply

wander and soak up the lively atmosphere (free entry!).

- **Tapas Hopping:** Embark on a culinary adventure by hopping between traditional tapas bars. Savor bite-sized delights like "patatas bravas" (spicy potatoes) or "croquetas" (creamy fried bites) while sharing stories and laughter with friends (tapas prices vary depending on the bar).
- **Paella Perfection:** Don't leave Valencia without trying an authentic paella, prepared with fresh seafood, rice, and vegetables. Head to local restaurants in neighborhoods like El Carmen or Ruzafa for the best flavors and experiences (prices vary depending on the restaurant).

Bonus:

- **Fallas Festival:** Witness the Las Fallas festival in March, a UNESCO-recognized celebration featuring giant satirical monuments and spectacular pyrotechnics. The city comes alive with music, parades, and a contagious festive spirit.
- **Feria de Julio:** Immerse yourself in the lively Feria de Julio in July, offering music, dance, bullfighting, and traditional Valencian culture.

Remember, Valencia is waiting to be explored! So pack your sense of adventure, your walking shoes, and your appetite, and get ready to discover the hidden gems and must-see marvels of this vibrant Spanish city.

Other Attractions
• **Torres de Quart (Quart Towers):** Impressive 14th-century gate towers offering city views (ticket: €2). Open Tuesday-Sunday 10:00-19:00.
• **Torres de Serrano (Serrano Towers):** Towering gate structures mirroring Torres de Quart, providing panoramic city views (ticket: €2). Open Tuesday-Sunday 10:00-19:00.

Historical Gems
1. El Carmen: Charming medieval neighborhood with narrow streets, colorful houses, and hidden plazas. Perfect for wandering and savoring tapas.
2. Ruzafa: Trendy and artistic district known for vibrant street art, independent shops, and trendy cafes.
3. Cabanyal: Maritime charm in a traditional fisherman's neighborhood. Stroll along the beach, enjoy fresh seafood, and visit the Las Arenas bullring.
4. L'Almoina Archaeological Site: Explore remains of Roman, Visigoth, and Islamic settlements beneath the city (ticket: €2). Open Tuesday-Sunday 10:00-19:00.

5. Serranos Palace: Magnificent 15th-century palace showcasing Valencian Gothic architecture and housing the Museum of Fine Arts (ticket: €2). Open Tuesday-Saturday 10:00-19:00, Sundays 10:00-14:00.

Beyond the Tourist Trail:
1. Jardín Botánico: Peaceful Botanical Gardens with diverse plant collections (free admission). Open Monday-Sunday 10:00-19:00 (winter) or 10:00-20:00 (summer).

2. Turia Gardens: Expansive urban park built over the former Turia Riverbed. Ideal for cycling, picnicking, and relaxation (free admission, open 24/7).

3. Bioparc Valencia: Unique zoo experience with animals roaming freely in recreated natural habitats (ticket: €24 adults, €18 children). Open daily 10:00-18:00.

4. Oceanogràfic: Spectacular aquarium showcasing marine life (€35 adults, €25 children). Open daily 10:00-18:00.

5. Ciudad de las Artes y las Ciencias (City of Arts and Sciences): Futuristic architectural complex with iconic structures and science exhibitions. Opening hours vary.

6. El Saler Beach: Pristine beach with soft sand, clear waters, and natural dunes. Perfect for swimming and water sports (free admission).

7. Albufera Natural Park: UNESCO World Heritage Site with Spain's largest freshwater lake. Explore by boat tour or hike (boat tours from €15).

Pro tip! Purchasing a Valencia Tourist Card is indeed a smart move for travelers. It not only provides cost savings on entry to major attractions but also offers the convenience of free public transportation and additional benefits. Enjoy your trip to Valencia, and make the most of the perks with your tourist card!

Cultural Immersion

Explore beyond Valencia's breathtaking landmarks; discover its vibrant culture, rich history, and lively celebrations. From perusing fascinating museums to indulging in local festivals, prepare for a journey that goes beyond typical sightseeing, immersing you in the heart of this captivating city.

Artistic Explorations:

- **Fine Arts Museum (Museo de Bellas Artes):** Immerse yourself in Spanish art, appreciating masterpieces by El Greco, Goya, and Sorolla (€2).

- **National Museum of Ceramics and Decorative Arts (Museo Nacional de Cerámica y Artes Decorativas):** Uncover Valencian craftsmanship with exquisite ceramics, furniture, and textiles (€2).
- **Valencian Institute of Modern Art (IVAM):** Explore contemporary art in a 17th-century palace, showcasing works by Spanish and international artists (€6).
- **Fallas Museum (Museo Fallero):** Dive into the world of Fallas, Valencia's iconic festival, through captivating exhibits and giant papier-mâché figures (€2).

Festival Delights:

- **Las Fallas (March):** Experience a spectacular festival of creativity and fire, witnessing satirical monuments before they're set ablaze during the "Nit de la Cremà."
- **July Fair (Feria de Julio):** Join month-long summer festivities with vibrant street parties, concerts, and bullfights.
- **Tomatina (August):** Engage in the messy fun of the world-famous tomato fight in the nearby town of Buñol.

- **Corpus Christi (June):** Witness elaborate floral carpets gracing the city streets during this religious festival.

Local Immersions:

1 Master the Art of Paella: Unleash your inner chef and learn the secrets of crafting authentic Valencian paella from scratch. Join a fun and interactive cooking class where you'll chop fresh ingredients, master traditional techniques, and finally, savor the delicious fruits of your labor.

Price: Expect a range of €30-€80 per person, depending on the provider and duration of the class.

Location: Many cooking classes are located in the central Ruzafa district, offering easy access to fresh ingredients and a vibrant atmosphere. Popular options include:
• **Ruzafa Cooking**
• **My First Paella**
• **Paella Valenciana**

2. Feel the Rhythm of Flamenco: Witness the captivating intensity of traditional flamenco dance at a local tablao. Be swept away by the rhythmic footwork, soulful singing, and expressive gestures that tell stories of love, loss, and cultural pride.

Price: Ticket prices vary depending on the venue and performance time, typically between €15-€40 per person.

Location: Tablao venues can be found throughout the city, particularly in the historic El Carmen and Ruzafa districts. Popular options include:

- **Tablao El Flamenco**
- **Casa de la Danza**
- **Torres Bermejas**

3. Sip on Refreshing Horchata: Escape the summer heat with a taste of Valencia's iconic horchata, a creamy and refreshing beverage made from tiger nuts. Visit a traditional horchatería, where the drink is made fresh daily and served alongside sweet pastries like fartons.

Price: A glass of horchata typically costs between €2-€4.

Location: Horchaterías are scattered throughout the city, often concentrated in historic areas like the central market and the Ciutat Vella district. Some famous spots include:

- **Horchatería Santa Catalina**
- **Horchatería Daniel**
- **Horchatería El Siglo**

4. Craft Beer Adventure: Embark on a journey through Valencia's burgeoning craft beer scene. Sample unique brews, learn about the brewing process directly from local artisans, and discover hidden gems off the beaten path.

Price: Prices vary depending on the tour length and included tastings, typically between €25-€50 per person.

Location: Several companies offer craft beer tours, often starting in the Ruzafa or Ciutat Vella districts and visiting breweries in different parts of the city. Popular options include:
- **Valencia Beer Tours**
- **Valencia Food Tours**
- **Devour Valencia**

5. Pedal Through the City: Discover Valencia's hidden alleyways, charming squares, and vibrant neighborhoods on two wheels. Take a leisurely bike tour with knowledgeable guides who will share insights into local culture and history.

Price: Bike rentals are available for around €10-€20 per day, while guided tours typically cost between €25-€40 per person.

Location: Bike rental shops can be found throughout the city, particularly near major tourist attractions and central areas. Recommended spots include:

50

- **Valenbisi**
- **Valencia Bikes**
- **Rent a Bike Valencia**

Pro Tip: Catch the electrifying atmosphere of a local sporting event, especially a Valencia CF football match at the Mestalla stadium. Witness the passionate support of the fans and experience the unique energy of Spanish sports culture.

Traveler's Reminders:
- Respect local customs and traditions during festivals and celebrations.
- Support local businesses and artisans by shopping at traditional markets and independent shops.
- Learn basic Spanish phrases to enhance communication with locals.
- Embrace the spirit of cultural discovery and be open to trying new experiences.

Beyond the City

Valencia's vibrant energy extends beyond its city limits, offering a myriad of day trips and weekend getaways to enchanting towns, stunning beaches, and breathtaking natural wonders. Get ready to escape the urban hustle and uncover hidden gems waiting to be explored:

Coastal Retreats:

1. Jávea & Denia: Enjoy golden sands at Jávea's cove beaches and explore its historic old town. In Denia, visit the Marina El Portet and the bustling fish market. Indulge in fresh seafood at harbor-front restaurants. (Distance: ~100km, 1h drive)

2. Cullera: Relax on the family-friendly Playa de Cullera beach, explore the medieval Cullera Castle for stunning views, and partake in watersports or sunbathe. (Distance: ~35km, 40min drive)

3. Sagunto & Malvarrosa Beach: Combine history at Sagunto's Roman ruins with a visit to the popular Malvarrosa Beach in Valencia. Explore the Sagunto Theatre and the charming old town. (Distance: ~20km, 25min drive)

Nature's Haven:

1. Albufera Natural Park: Discover Spain's largest freshwater lake on boat tours, hike or bike through rice fields, and explore the traditional farming practices. (Distance: ~10km, 20min drive)

2. Sierra Calderona Natural Park: Hike or bike through pine forests, uncover hidden waterfalls like Salto de la Garrofera, and enjoy panoramic views from Pico del Garbí. (Distance: ~25km, 30min drive)

3. Montanejos: Immerse yourself in a natural oasis with waterfalls like Salto de la Chorra, relax in thermal springs, and engage in adventure activities. (Distance: ~65km, 1h drive)

Charming Towns & Historical Gems:

1. Xàtiva: Explore Valencia's history at the Alcazaba fortress, Santa María Cathedral, and indulge in local turrón. (Distance: ~50km, 50min drive)

2. Guadalest: Visit the medieval castle, wander through narrow streets lined with shops, and enjoy breathtaking views of the Guadalest Valley. (Distance: ~75km, 1h 15min drive)

3. Altea & Peníscola: Discover artistic Altea with its whitewashed houses and visit the medieval Peníscola with its imposing castle. (Distance: ~120km, 1h 45min drive)

Pro Tip: Consider renting a car for flexibility on day trips. Public transportation is available for some destinations like Sagunto and Cullera.

Remember:
- Pack accordingly for your activity—swimwear, hiking boots, or comfortable shoes.
- Research opening hours and entrance fees, especially in peak season.
- Respect the local environment and embrace

nature, history, and culture beyond the city.

Venture beyond Valencia to uncover diverse hidden gems, each offering a unique experience.

Activities for Everyone

Valencia caters to diverse interests, offering something for everyone, from families seeking fun excursions to foodies craving culinary adventures, and history buffs yearning for cultural immersion. Let's explore activities tailored to your unique preferences:

For Families:
- **Oceanogràfic:** Dive into the underwater world at this spectacular aquarium, showcasing diverse marine life from the Mediterranean, Arctic, and tropical regions (€35 adults, €25 children). Witness playful dolphins, majestic sharks, and colorful coral reefs across diverse ecosystems.
- **Bioparc Valencia:** Immerse yourselves in a unique zoo experience, where animals roam freely in recreated natural habitats (€24 adults, €18 children). Spot lions basking in the sun, giraffes reaching for leaves, and playful monkeys swinging through trees.

- **Ciudad de las Artes y las Ciencias:** Explore this futuristic architectural complex, featuring interactive exhibits and attractions like the Hemisfèric (IMAX cinema and planetarium) and the Science Museum (individual ticket prices vary). Learn about space exploration, the human body, and more through fun and engaging experiences.
- **Gulliver Park:** Let your little ones loose in this giant Gulliver-themed playground, featuring slides, climbing structures, and swings (€2.50 entry). While the kids play, adults can relax in the surrounding gardens or enjoy a picnic lunch.
- **Valencia Boat Tour:** Embark on a scenic cruise along the Turia River, offering stunning views of the city's landmarks like the City of Arts and Sciences and the Torres de Quart (€15 adults, €10 children). Enjoy live commentary and learn about Valencia's history and culture.

For Foodies:
- **Paella Cooking Class:** Learn the art of preparing this iconic Valencian dish from scratch, enjoying the fruits of your labor afterwards (prices vary depending on location and duration). Discover the secrets behind the perfect paella and impress your friends and family back home.
- **Central Market:** Immerse yourself in the sights, sounds, and aromas of this vibrant market, dating

back to 1928. Peruse stalls overflowing with fresh produce, local delicacies like paella and horchata, and handcrafted souvenirs. Enjoy tapas at nearby bars or indulge in a picnic lunch in the Turia Gardens.

• **Wine Tasting in Utiel-Requena:** Embark on a day trip to the Utiel-Requena wine region, known for its Bobal grapes and unique Denominación de Origen (DO). Visit wineries for tastings and guided tours, learning about the winemaking process and savoring the local flavors (€20-€50 per winery).

• **Tapas Crawl:** Immerse yourself in the local culinary scene with a tapas crawl through the El Carmen or Ruzafa neighborhoods. Sample a variety of small plates at different bars, enjoying the vibrant atmosphere and delicious food (prices vary depending on bars and tapas chosen).

• **Chocolate Tour:** Discover Valencia's rich chocolate tradition with a guided tour of a historic chocolate factory (Chocolatería Valor) or a tasting session at a local shop (prices vary). Learn about the bean-to-bar process and indulge in decadent treats.

For Adventure Seekers:
• **Hiking in Sierra Calderona Natural Park:** Explore scenic trails amidst pine forests, offering stunning views of the surrounding mountains. Hike

to the peak of Pico del Garbí, the highest point in the park, and enjoy panoramic vistas. (Free entrance, various hiking routes available)

• **Kayaking on the Albufera:** Paddle through the diverse ecosystem of Spain's largest freshwater lake, observing birdlife and enjoying the tranquility of nature. Kayaking tours are available for different skill levels (prices vary depending on duration and provider).

• **Caving in Cullera:** Embark on a guided spelunking adventure in the Cueva del Parpalló, discovering ancient cave paintings and fossils dating back thousands of years (tour prices vary).

• **Rock Climbing in Montanejos:** Challenge yourself on climbing routes of varying difficulty in the scenic Montanejos gorge. Experienced climbers can attempt challenging ascents, while beginners can enjoy introductory sessions with qualified guides (prices vary depending on experience and duration).

• **Windsurfing or Kitesurfing in Cullera:** Catch some waves and enjoy the thrill of windsurfing or kitesurfing on the Playa de Cullera beach. Lessons and equipment rentals are available for all levels (prices vary depending on provider and duration).

For History Buffs:
• **Valencia Cathedral:** Explore this majestic Gothic cathedral, construction beginning in 1262, and marvel at its diverse architectural styles. Climb the Miguelete Bell Tower for panoramic views (€2) and witness the Holy Grail (free admission).
• **La Lonja de la Seda (Silk Exchange):** Uncover the secrets of Valencia's silk trade at this UNESCO World Heritage Site, built in the 15th century.

Hidden Gems

Discover Valencia's hidden gems, revealing the city's authentic character, unique traditions, and captivating stories. Put on your explorer hat and venture off the beaten path:

For the Art Enthusiast:
1. IVAM Institut Valencià d'Art Modern: Immerse yourself in contemporary art, exploring works by Spanish and international artists (€6). Dive into exhibits featuring photography, installations, and multimedia art. (Location: Carrer Guillem de Castro, 118, 46003 València)

2. Ceramic Museum of l'Alcora: Delve into Valencian ceramics' rich history and intricate craftsmanship at this charming museum in l'Alcora (€2). Explore collections spanning centuries, showcasing exquisite tableware and decorative tiles. (Location: Plaça de l'Església, 6, 12110 l'Alcora)

3. Graffiti & Street Art Tour: Uncover vibrant street art murals reflecting Valencia's urban culture and social commentary on a guided walking tour through alternative neighborhoods like Ruzafa and Cabanyal (prices vary). (Start points vary depending on tour operator; inquire for specific locations)

For the Nature Lover:

1. Jardí Botànic de la Universitat de València: Escape the city at the peaceful Botanical Gardens of the University of Valencia. Stroll amidst diverse plant collections, including a rose garden and a palm grove (free admission). (Location: Av. dels Tarongers, s/n, 46010 València)

2. Jardín del Palau de la Música: Discover a hidden oasis within the City of Arts and Sciences. This serene garden features water features, lush vegetation, and sculptures, offering a haven for relaxation (free admission). (Location: Av. Professor López Piñero, 7, 46013 València)

3. Albufera Natural Park at Night: Experience the mesmerizing bioluminescence phenomenon on a guided night tour of the Albufera Natural Park, kayaking through illuminated waters (prices vary). (Location: Tours depart from various points near the Albufera Natural Park; inquire for specific details)

For the Foodie
1. Horchatería Vida: Indulge in the authentic taste of horchata at this traditional horchatería since 1909. Enjoy the creamy drink with sweet pastries or "fartons" (long, spongey biscuits). (Location: Carrer de Sorní, 15, 46003 València)
2. Central Market after Hours: Explore the market after closing hours with a "gastro tour." Sample local delicacies, learn about Valencian cuisine, and soak up the unique atmosphere (prices vary). (Location: Central Market, Plaça de la Ciutat de Bruges, s/n, 46003 València)
3. Tapas in Ruzafa: Discover hidden tapas bars in the trendy Ruzafa neighborhood, offering creative plates paired with local craft beers or Valencian wines (prices vary). (Start point: Ruzafa neighborhood, specific bar recommendations online or through local food blogs)

For the History Buff
1. El Almudín: Uncover Valencia's maritime trade history at this 14th-century grain exchange building. Explore Gothic architecture and exhibits

showcasing ancient weights, measures, coins, and maritime tools (free admission). (Location: Plaça de la Ciutat de Bruges, s/n, 46003 València)

2. Monasterio de San Miguel de los Reyes: Step back in time at this Renaissance monastery with intricate architecture, cloisters, ornate frescoes, and sculptures (free admission). (Location: Carrer del Monestir, 9, 46014 València)

3. Basílica de San Vicente Ferrer: Visit the grand basilica dedicated to Saint Vincent Ferrer, marveling at its Baroque architecture, including the impressive dome and decorative altars (free admission). (Location: Plaça de Sant Vicent Ferrer, 46002 València)

CHAPTER 5: SAVOURING VALENCIA

Delight in Valencia's vibrant culinary scene, where traditional dishes and local specialties take center stage, offering a diverse and rich gastronomic experience:

Traditional Dishes

1. Paella: The iconic Valencian rice dish, featuring chicken, rabbit, and local white beans (garrofó). Variations include seafood and vegetarian options (€15-€30+ per person, available throughout Valencia).

2. Fideuà: A flavorful dish similar to paella but with thin noodles, often prepared with seafood (€18-€25+ per person, primarily found in coastal regions).

3. All i pebre: A comforting dish with chicken or rabbit cooked in garlic, paprika, and tomatoes (€12-€18+ per person, widely available in Valencia).

4. Clóchinas: Locally-sourced mussels steamed or grilled, perfect as a light appetizer (€5-€10, popular in coastal areas).

5. Arroz al horno: A baked rice dish with chicken, sausages, and rosemary, offering a hearty flavor (€15-€25+ per person, found throughout Valencia).

Must-Try Local Specialties:

1. Horchata: A refreshing beverage made from tiger nuts, best enjoyed with traditional "fartons" (€2-€4 per glass, widespread in horchaterías).
2. Turrón: Quintessential Valencian nougat available in various flavors (prices vary, found in dedicated shops and markets).
3. Agua de Valencia: A refreshing cava-based cocktail with orange juice and brandy (€5-€8 per glass, popular in bars during summer).
4. Espardenyà: Wheat flour and olive oil flatbread served with tomatoes and garlic (€4-€6 per serving, found in local restaurants).
5. Xocolata: Indulge in Valencian chocolate tradition, especially churros con chocolate (€3-€5 for churros, €2-€4 for hot chocolate, available in chocolaterías and cafes).

Unveiling culinary gems

Immerse yourself in the authentic flavors of the region. Here's a recap of the culinary treasures awaiting your discovery in Valencia:

In Ruzafa:

1. Bar El Maño: Creative tapas using seasonal ingredients. Budget-friendly at around €2-€4 per tapa (Location: Carrer de Sueca, 46, 46006 València).

In Cabanyal:

2. La Cuina de Carmen: Family-run restaurant offering classic dishes like paella valenciana. Main courses range from €18-€25 (Location: Carrer de Barraques, 123, 46011 València).

Fine Dining:

3. Canela: Michelin-starred restaurant with a modern approach to Valencian cuisine. Tasting menus priced around €150 and upwards (Location: Carrer dels Àngels, 10, 46002 València).

City Center:

4. Central Bar: Vibrant tapas bar with traditional and innovative options. Prices typically range from €3-€6 per tapa (Location: Carrer de la Corona, 39, 46002 València).

Historic Market:

5. Mercado de Colón: Gourmet food hall with diverse culinary options. Prices vary depending on the vendor and dish (Location: Carrer de Jorge Juan, 19, 46003 València).

Additional Hidden Gems

6. Casa Isabel: Old Town restaurant with over 100

years of history. Traditional Valencian dishes range from €15-€25 per main course (Location: Carrer de les Basses, 10, 46003 València).

7. Bodega La Cigarra: Traditional "bodega" in the Carmen neighborhood with local wines and budget-friendly tapas (Location: Carrer de la Reina, 10, 46003 València).

8. El Bouet: Beachside restaurant in Malvarrosa offering fresh seafood. Main course prices typically range from €25-€40+ (Location: Passeig Marítim de la Patacona, 58, 46117 València).

9. Bar Ricardo: Family-run restaurant in Ruzafa with authentic Valencian cuisine. Main courses are moderately priced, ranging from €12-€20 (Location: Carrer de Sueca, 44, 46006 València).

Remember to explore local markets, ask locals for recommendations, and consider food tours to enhance your culinary exploration in Valencia. Venture beyond the usual spots, and let the city's hidden culinary gems unfold before you.

Food Tours and Markets

Valencia's culinary scene bursts with flavors, presenting a delightful blend of traditional dishes, fresh local produce, and innovative creations. To fully engage in this dynamic food culture, consider navigating the city through guided food tours and lively markets.

Food Tours:

Unearth the mysteries of Valencian cuisine by participating in a guided food tour, delving into the city's culinary history and traditions. These tours lead you through the historic center, stopping at hidden gems and renowned restaurants for authentic samplings of dishes like paella, fideuà, and tapas. Many tours also incorporate visits to local markets, providing insights into the fresh ingredients foundational to Valencian cuisine. Prices for food tours typically range from €50-€100+ per person, contingent on duration, inclusions, and the specific company.

How to Join a Food Tour:

1. Research Online: Utilize various platforms such as Viator, Get Your Guide, Airbnb Experiences, and local tour operators' websites for booking food tours in Valencia.

2. Review and Compare: Opt for tours with favorable ratings and feedback, considering factors like price, itinerary, inclusions (meals, tastings, drinks), and duration.

3. Book Online: Once you've selected a tour, complete the online booking process, ensuring comprehension of cancellation policies and payment terms.

4. Confirmation: Many companies will send a confirmation email with details about the meeting point, necessary items, and contact information.

Markets:

1. Central Market (Mercat Central):
- **Location:** Iconic market in a modernist building.
- **Highlights:** Colorful stalls offering fresh produce, seafood, meats, cheeses, and local delicacies.
- **Must-Try:** Freshly squeezed orange juice, a Valencian staple.

2. Ruzafa Market (Mercat de Ruzafa):
- **Location:** Trendy Ruzafa neighborhood.
- **Offerings:** Mix of traditional and modern food stalls featuring fresh produce, local specialties like horchata and turrón, and international delicacies.

3. Colon Market (Mercado de Colón):
- **Location:** Gourmet food hall in a beautifully restored Art Nouveau building.
- **Attractions:** Array of restaurants and stalls showcasing the best of Valencian cuisine, offering tapas, paella, fresh seafood, and more.

Additional Tips:
- Book your food tour in advance, especially during peak seasons.
- Consider a private tour for a personalized experience tailored to your interests.
- Dress comfortably for walking and exploring.
- Bring cash, as some smaller stalls may only accept cash.
- Embrace the adventure and savor the unique flavors of Valencia's vibrant food scene.

Wine and Drinks

Valencia, beyond its captivating beaches and dynamic culture, possesses a rich winemaking legacy and a diverse beverage scene awaiting exploration. From globally acclaimed wines to refreshing local drinks, here's a guide to entice your taste buds:

Wines

Utiel-Requena: Situated northwest of Valencia, this Denominación de Origen (DO) is famed for its Bobal grape, yielding bold red wines with hints of black fruit and spice. Explore varietals like Tempranillo, Garnacha, and Chardonnay, available in styles from dry to sweet. (Prices typically range from €10-€30+ per bottle, depending on the specific wine and vintage. Many restaurants offer these wines by the glass for €5-€10+.)

Valencia DO: Encompassing diverse wine styles from the Valencian region, this broader DO introduces red, white, rosé, and sparkling wines (Cava) crafted from local grape varieties like Merseguera, Macabeo, and Garnacha Tintorera. (Prices typically fall in the €8-€25+ per bottle range, depending on the specific wine and vintage. Restaurants offer them by the glass for €4-€8+.)

Visiting Wineries

Immerse yourself in the winemaking process by visiting a winery in the Utiel-Requena or Valencia DOs. Many wineries offer tours, tastings, and the chance to purchase bottles directly from the source. (Tour and tasting prices typically range from €15-€30+ per person, depending on the winery and inclusions.)

Local Drinks

Horchata: Crafted from tiger nuts (chufa), this refreshing beverage presents a unique and slightly sweet flavor. Enjoy it solo or paired with traditional "fartons" (long, spongey biscuits) for a delightful treat. (Expect to pay around €2-€4 per glass of horchata and €1-€2 per farton, available in horchaterías, cafes, and markets throughout Valencia.)

Agua de Valencia: A refreshing cocktail perfect for warm summer days, Agua de Valencia combines cava (Spanish sparkling wine), orange juice, and brandy, boasting a potent flavor. (Prices typically fall in the €5-€8 range per glass, found in bars, restaurants, and cafes, particularly popular during summer months.)

Café Bombón: This Valencian specialty, a "coffee bomb," merges espresso with condensed milk, creating a sweet and creamy treat. (Expect to pay around €2-€3 per cup, found in cafes, bars, and restaurants throughout Valencia.)

Cremaet: A traditional after-dinner drink featuring rum, coffee, lemon rind, and cinnamon, often served flambéed for a dramatic presentation. (Priced around €4-€6 per serving, found in restaurants, often on dessert menus.)

Exploring the Beverage Scene
Wine Bars

Valencia boasts numerous wine bars offering a diverse selection of local and international wines by the glass or bottle. These establishments often serve tapas, creating a perfect pairing for your wine exploration. Popular areas for wine bars include Ruzafa and El Carmen. (Wine prices can vary, but expect to pay around €4-€8+ per glass and €20-€40+ per bottle, with tapas typically ranging from €2-€6 each.)

Restaurants:
Many restaurants in Valencia showcase local wines alongside their menu, allowing you to pair your meal with the perfect regional grape. (Wine prices in restaurants typically fall in line with the information provided for wine bars.)

Bodegas:
These traditional taverns offer a more casual atmosphere, serving local wines, beers, and simple tapas at affordable prices. (Expect to pay around €2-€4 per glass of wine, €1-€3 for beers, and €2-€5 for tapas, found throughout the city, particularly in neighborhoods like El Carmen and El Cabanyal.)

Additional Tips:
- **Ask for recommendations:** Local bartenders and restaurant staff are often passionate about their city's wine and beverage scene. Don't hesitate to ask for their recommendations based on your preferences.
- **Attend a wine festival:** If you're visiting during specific times of the year, consider attending a wine festival like the "Feria del Vino de Utiel-Requena"

or the "Fiesta de la Vendimia" (Grape Harvest Festival) for a truly immersive experience.

- Learn some basic Spanish phrases: Knowing a few basic phrases like "un vaso de..." (a glass of...) or "me gusta..." (I like...) can help you navigate the local beverage scene and ensure a more enjoyable experience.

CHAPTER 6: PRACTICAL INFORMATION

Money Matters

When planning a trip to Valencia, ensure a seamless experience by considering various financial aspects beyond flights and accommodation:

Currency Exchange:

- **Currency:** Euro (€) is the official currency in Spain, including Valencia.
- **Exchange Rates:** Research current rates for informed spending decisions using online tools or mobile apps.
- **Exchanging Money:** Options include airports, banks, exchange bureaus, or ATMs. Compare rates and fees, and consider withdrawal charges.
- **Travel Cards:** Pre-paid travel cards offer convenience and security with competitive rates but may have additional fees

Budgeting Tips:

- **Accommodation:** Choose from budget-friendly hostels to luxury apartments, considering location and amenities.
- **Food and Drinks:** Save by exploring local markets, supermarkets, and budget-friendly restaurants. Cafes and tapas bars offer affordable snacks and drinks.
- **Transportation:** Opt for efficient and affordable public transport, walking, or cycling to explore the city inexpensively.
- **Activities:** Enjoy free activities and selectively choose paid ones based on interests and budget.
- Souvenirs: Opt for locally-made items for better value and to support local businesses.

Accepted Payment Methods:

- **Cash:** Still widely accepted, especially at smaller establishments.
- **Credit and Debit Cards:** Visa, Mastercard, and Maestro are widely accepted; check international transaction fees.
- **Contactless Payments:** Increasingly popular, ensure your cards and devices are contactless-enabled.

Additional Tips

- **Tipping:** While not mandatory, a small tip (5-10%) is appreciated in restaurants and taxis.
- **Tax Refunds:** Purchases exceeding a certain amount may be eligible for VAT refunds; inquire at the store.
- **Bargaining:** Uncommon in most places, but possible at flea markets or with street vendors; be respectful.

Communication

Staying connected in Valencia is crucial for getting around the city, translating info, and sharing your adventures with folks back home. Here's what you should keep in mind:

Wi-Fi Access

- **Free Wi-Fi:** Many spots in Valencia offer free Wi-Fi, like libraries, museums, parks, squares, and even the beach. Keep an eye out for the "WiFiValencia" network or inquire at local establishments.
- **Accommodation:** Most hotels, hostels, and guesthouses provide Wi-Fi as part of their services.
- **Cafes and Restaurants:** Plenty of cafes and restaurants have Wi-Fi for customers, sometimes with a purchase requirement.

- **Mobile Data:** Using your phone's data plan can be pricey, especially with international roaming charges. Consider grabbing a local SIM card with a data package for more budget-friendly connectivity.

Phone Cards

- **Prepaid SIM Cards:** Various mobile operators in Spain offer prepaid SIM cards with data plans and calling options. Popular choices include Orange, Movistar, and Vodafone. Check out different plans and prices before making a decision.
- **Activate International Roaming:** If you prefer using your home phone plan, activate international roaming before your trip. Be mindful of potential high roaming charges.

Basic Spanish Phrases

- **Greetings:** Hey (Hello), Good morning (Buenos días), Good afternoon (Buenas tardes), Good evening (Buenas noches), Bye (Adiós).
- **Essential Phrases:** Do you speak English? (¿Habla inglés?), Please (Por favor), Thank you (Gracias), I'm sorry (Lo siento), How much does this cost? (¿Cuánto cuesta esto?), Where is…? (¿Dónde está…?)

- **Food and Drinks:** One coffee, please (Un café, por favor), I would like... (Me gustaría...), Do you have...? (¿Tiene...?), The bill, please (La cuenta, por favor).
- **Numbers:** One (Uno), Two (Dos), Three (Tres), Four (Cuatro), Five (Cinco), Six (Seis), Seven (Siete), Eight (Ocho), Nine (Nueve), Ten (Diez).

Additional Tips

- **Download translation apps:** Apps like Google Translate can be handy for quick translations and basic communication.
- **Learn basic pronunciation:** Knowing how to pronounce basic Spanish words can enhance communication and show locals you're making an effort.
- **Be patient and respectful:** Some locals might not speak English fluently, so be patient and respectful when communicating.
- **Use gestures and body language:** Feel free to use gestures and body language to help get your point across.

Safety and Security

Ensuring a secure and worry-free trip to Valencia is paramount for a positive experience. Here are key safety tips to keep in mind:

General Safety

- **Stay vigilant:** Be attentive to your surroundings, particularly in crowded areas. Secure valuables like wallets and phones in bags with closures or concealed pockets.

- **Nighttime precautions:** Opt for well-lit and populated routes after dark. Consider using a taxi or ride-sharing app if walking alone at night.

- **Trust your instincts:** If a situation feels unsafe, steer clear. Seek assistance from locals, police, or hotel staff without hesitation.

- **Guard against pickpockets:** Especially in tourist-heavy spots, be mindful of pickpockets. Keep belongings close and avoid displaying valuables openly.

- **Respect local customs:** Understand local laws and customs to prevent misunderstandings. Dress modestly at religious sites and be mindful of noise levels in public spaces.

Emergency Numbers

- **Emergency Services:** Dial 112 for all emergencies, including police, ambulance, and fire department.

- **Local Police:** Call 092 for non-emergency situations.

- **National Police:** In serious emergencies, dial 091.
- **Tourist Police:** For English-speaking assistance, contact 902 10 12 34.

Scams to Avoid

- **Ticket scams:** Purchase tickets only from authorized vendors to avoid counterfeits.
- **Fake taxis:** Stick to licensed taxis or reputable ride-sharing apps with visible licenses and meters.
- **Friendship scams:** Exercise caution with fast-forming friendships, as they may lead to theft or scams.
- **Overpriced goods/services:** Be wary of significantly inflated prices; compare before making purchases.

Additional Tips:

- **Get travel insurance:** Ensure coverage for unexpected events like medical emergencies or trip cancellations.
- **Duplicate important documents:** Keep copies of vital documents separate from originals.
- **Register with your embassy:** Registration provides assistance during emergencies or passport loss.

Sustainable Travel

Embracing its goal to become a European Green Capital in 2024, Valencia invites like-minded travelers who value sustainability and responsible tourism. Here are ways you can actively participate in a greener and more positive travel experience:

Eco-Friendly Practices

Transportation:
- **Walk, cycle, or use public transport:** Valencia's well-connected and affordable network includes buses, trams, and metro lines.
- **Minimize taxi rides:** Opt for public transport or eco-friendly ride-sharing apps.
- **Choose electric taxis or carpooling:** Explore electric taxi services or carpooling options for environmentally conscious journeys.

Accommodation:
- **Select eco-certified hotels:** Look for eco-labels like LEED or Green Globe, indicating a commitment to sustainability.
- **Conserve water and energy:** Practice mindful water and energy usage, including short showers and turning off unused lights and air conditioning.
- **Minimize single-use plastics:** Carry a reusable

water bottle and shopping bag to reduce plastic waste.

Responsible Tourism Options
- **Support local businesses:** Prioritize local markets, restaurants, and shops to boost the local economy and preserve culture.
- **Respect the environment:** Dispose of waste responsibly, refrain from littering, and show consideration for local flora and fauna.
- **Engage with cultural experiences:** Immerse yourself in local culture through museums, festivals, and traditional activities.
- **Choose responsible tours and activities:** Opt for eco-tourism tours or ethical animal experiences.

Additional Tips
- **Minimize food waste:** Order conservatively, compost food scraps, and avoid buffet-style meals to reduce food wastage.
- **Donate to local environmental organizations:** Support local initiatives focused on environmental conservation or sustainability.
- **Learn about local sustainability efforts:** Understand Valencia's Green Capital initiatives and contribute during your visit.
- **Spread awareness:** Share your sustainable

practices with fellow travelers and encourage a collective commitment.

- **Leave no trace:** Adhere to the "leave no trace" principle by minimizing your environmental impact.

By embracing these eco-friendly practices and responsible tourism options, you actively contribute to Valencia's sustainable future and ensure a fulfilling travel experience. Small changes can lead to significant positive impacts, so be a mindful and responsible traveler, leaving a lasting positive impression on this beautiful city.

CHAPTER 7: FINDING THE BEST TRAVEL DEALS

Valencia warmly welcomes travelers with diverse budgets, providing opportunities to savor its charm even with limited spending. Here are tips to uncover the best travel deals and make your budget go further:

Finding Affordable Flights

- **Be flexible with travel dates:** Opt for shoulder seasons for lower airfares.
- **Compare flight options:** Use online aggregators like Skyscanner or Kayak to compare prices across multiple platforms.
- **Set price alerts:** Stay informed when prices drop by setting up alerts for your preferred route.
- **Consider budget airlines:** Explore no-frills options for potentially lower costs.
- **Look for deals and promotions:** Subscribe to newsletters and follow airlines on social media for exclusive offers.

Finding Affordable Accommodation:

- **Explore alternative options:** Consider hostels, guesthouses, or vacation rentals for budget-friendly stays.
- **Book in advance:** Secure better deals by booking accommodation in advance, especially during peak seasons.
- **Look for discounts:** Many providers offer discounts for seniors, students, or longer stays.
- **Stay outside the city center:** Choose neighborhoods slightly outside the central area for more affordable options.
- **Take advantage of free cancellation policies:** Opt for accommodations with flexible cancellation policies.

Finding Affordable Activities:

- **Enjoy free activities:** Explore parks, visit museums on free days, stroll along the beach, or attend outdoor markets.
- **Discounted passes:** Purchase city passes or discount cards for reduced prices at multiple attractions.

- **Look for deals:** Many attractions offer online booking discounts, early bird tickets, or specific day promotions.
- **Attend free events:** Check local listings for free cultural events, concerts, or festivals during your stay.
- **Seek alternative experiences:** Opt for free walking tours, explore local neighborhoods, or have a picnic in a park.

Additional Tips:
- **Cook some meals yourself:** Utilize self-catering options in vacation rentals or hostels.
- **Pack light:** Avoid baggage fees by packing light and using public transportation.
- **Drink tap water:** Save on bottled water costs by enjoying safe tap water.
- **Use free Wi-Fi:** Stay connected without data roaming charges in cafes, libraries, and public spaces.
- **Travel off-peak:** Visit attractions during off-peak hours for shorter queues and potentially lower fees.

Remember, strategic planning and exploring alternatives allow you to create lasting memories on a budget-friendly trip to Valencia without compromising your experience.

Budgeting Strategies

Sure, you could blow your entire travel fund on fancy tapas and flamenco shows, but where's the adventure in that? Valencia is bursting with hidden gems and budget-friendly fun waiting to be discovered. So ditch the fear of missing out and let's unlock the secrets to an epic Valencia trip without breaking the bank!

First things first: Let's talk moolah. Before you even book that flight, set a realistic budget that covers everything from sky monsters (aka airplanes) and cozy crash pads to delicious eats and unforgettable adventures. Prioritize the experiences that make your heart sing, whether it's scaling the Miguelete bell tower for panoramic views or getting lost in the vibrant Central Market. Remember, every saved euro is another glass of horchata (trust me, you'll thank me later!).

Flight Fight Club: Outsmart those pesky airfare prices by being a travel ninja! Be flexible with dates, consider flying during the shoulder seasons (think spring or fall), and use price trackers to snag the best deals. Budget airlines might not offer in-flight massages, but they'll get you to Valencia with euros to spare for that extra churro.

Accomodation Showdown: Ditch the fancy hotels (unless your inner Kardashian is screaming) and explore hostels, guesthouses, or even vacation rentals. They're often cheaper, more social, and give you a taste of local life. Plus, cooking your own breakfast means more euros for paella, right?

Food Glorious Food: Valencia is a foodie paradise, but it doesn't have to cost a fortune. Hit up the local markets for fresh ingredients, grab a "menú del día" (a set lunch menu) for a steal, and don't be afraid to try street food – it's usually delicious and budget-friendly. Remember, sometimes the best meals are shared with newfound friends over laughter and a bottle of cheap-but-cheerful vino.

Activity All-Stars: Valencia is packed with free and affordable things to do. Get your nature fix in the Turia Gardens, explore stunning museums on free admission days, or join a free walking tour for insider tips. Remember, the best souvenirs are memories, not overpriced trinkets.

Transportation Tango: Ditch the taxis and embrace the awesome public transport system. Trams, buses, and the metro will whizz you around the city for a few euros. Feeling adventurous? Rent a bike and explore Valencia on two wheels – it's good for your wallet and your waistline!

Bonus Tip Jar: Pack light to avoid baggage fees, drink that delicious tap water (it's safe!), and utilize free Wi-Fi whenever possible. Every saved euro means more churros, more paella, more memories!

Remember, the best vacations aren't about spending the most, but experiencing the most. So, pack your sense of adventure, your haggling skills (for the markets!), and get ready to discover the magic of Valencia on a budget!

Free and Cheap Activities

Forget the fancy tapas and flamenco shows (although they do have their charm!), Valencia is your budget-savvy best friend. This sun-kissed city on Spain's Mediterranean coast is bursting with hidden gems and wallet-friendly adventures waiting to be discovered. So ditch the fear of missing out and get ready to unlock the secrets to an epic Valencia trip without breaking the bank!

Imagine strolling through vibrant green parks, getting lost in the maze of charming historical buildings, or building sandcastles on golden beaches – all without spending a dime. Valencia offers a treasure trove of free and cheap activities that will leave you with memories to last a lifetime.

Free and Fantastic

• **Park Perfection:** Breathe in the fresh air and soak up the sunshine at the Jardí del Turia, a sprawling urban oasis transformed from a former riverbed. Rent a bike, have a picnic under the palm trees, or simply relax and enjoy the peaceful atmosphere. It's the perfect escape from the hustle and bustle of the city.

• **Museum Marvels:** Dive into Valencia's rich history and culture at museums with free admission days or hours. Explore the Valencia History Museum, marvel at contemporary art at the IVAM, or get your science fix at the Principe Felipe Science Museum. Remember to check the schedules to plan your free museum explorations!

• **Market Magic:** Immerse yourself in the sights, smells, and lively buzz of the Central Market. Wander through stalls overflowing with fresh produce, local delicacies, and handcrafted souvenirs. It's a feast for the senses and a budget-friendly way to experience the city's vibrant culture.

• **Architectural Gems:** Valencia is an open-air museum of stunning architecture. Admire the majestic Valencia Cathedral, get lost in the charming El Carmen neighborhood, and be awestruck by the futuristic Ciudad de las Artes y las Ciencias complex. Whether you're an architecture buff or simply appreciate beautiful sights, Valencia has something to offer everyone.

• **Beach Bliss:** Feel the sand between your toes and the Mediterranean breeze in your hair at Playa de la Malvarrosa. Take a refreshing dip, build sandcastles with the kids, or relax with a good book and the sound of waves crashing. Remember, the beach is always a free and fabulous way to spend an afternoon.

Cheap and Cheerful:

• **Tapas Time:** Indulge in the quintessential Spanish experience – tapas hopping! Sample delicious bites at various bars, sharing plates with friends and experiencing the local culinary scene. Look for "menú del día" options for even better deals, often including a drink and dessert. Remember, tapas are meant to be social, so grab some friends and embark on a delicious culinary adventure!

• **Public Transport Prowess:** Get around the city like a local with Valencia's efficient public transport system. Purchase a T-Valencia card for unlimited rides on buses, trams, and the metro. It's affordable, convenient, and a great way to experience the city alongside friendly Valencians.

• **Walking Wanderings:** Lace up your shoes and explore Valencia's charming neighborhoods on foot. Get lost in the winding streets of the old town, discover hidden plazas, and stumble upon unexpected gems. It's a free and healthy way to soak up the local atmosphere, get some exercise, and save some euros while you're at it.

• **Festival Fun:** Throughout the year, Valencia comes alive with vibrant festivals and celebrations. From the colorful Las Fallas festival with its towering monuments to the lively Feria de Julio with music, dance, and fireworks, there's always something happening. Many of these events are free or have affordable entry fees, making them a perfect way to experience the city's culture without breaking the bank.

So, ditch the expensive tourist traps and embrace the spirit of adventure. Explore hidden corners, indulge in free delights, and let Valencia surprise you with its budget-friendly charm!

Eating Like a Local

Valencia's culinary scene beckons with fresh flavors, whispering the secrets of its rich history and Mediterranean bounty. But navigating this delicious maze can be tricky, especially if you're pinching pennies and want to avoid tourist traps. Don't worry, fellow budget-conscious gourmand! Follow this guide to eat like a local in Valencia, indulging in authentic dishes without breaking the bank.

Market Magic:

• **Central Market:** Dive into the sensory explosion of Valencia's iconic market. Feast your eyes on fresh produce, local delicacies, and handcrafted treats. Sample seasonal fruits, cured meats, and artisan cheeses for a delightful (and affordable!) snack.

• **El Cabanyal Market:** Experience the local rhythm at El Cabanyal. This traditional market offers fresh seafood straight from the sea, alongside regional specialties. Chat with friendly vendors and discover hidden gems like "clóchinas," small mussels bursting with flavor.

Tapas Time:

• **Bar Hopping Bliss:** Tapas hopping is a Spanish ritual, and Valencia does it right! Skip the main squares and explore neighborhoods like Ruzafa or El Carmen. Order small plates like "patatas bravas" (spicy potatoes), "croquetas" (creamy fried bites), or "boquerones en vinagre" (marinated anchovies) to share with friends. Savor each bite and enjoy the company.

Paella Perfection
• **Ditch the Tourist Traps:** Resist the overpriced paella in main squares. Seek out authentic restaurants frequented by locals. Look for places with wood-fired ovens and a focus on fresh, seasonal ingredients. Ask the staff for recommendations – they'll guide you towards the most delicious and budget-friendly options.

Lunchtime Delights
• **Menú del Día:** Embrace the "menú del día," a set lunch typically offering a starter, main course, dessert, and often a drink, all for a fixed price. This is a fantastic way to try local dishes at a fraction of the a la carte cost. Look for restaurants with handwritten menus, often indicating traditional fare.

Sweet Endings
• **Horchata Heaven:** Valencia's famous horchata, a refreshing and creamy drink made with tiger nuts, is a must-try. Skip the overpriced cafes and head to local "horchaterías" for an authentic and affordable taste of this Valencian specialty.

Turrón Temptation: Don't miss turrón, a traditional nougat candy available in various flavors and textures. Visit local shops or markets to find artisanal varieties at reasonable prices, perfect for souvenirs or sweet treats.

Bonus Tip: Join the "merienda" tradition, a mid-afternoon snack around 5 pm. Grab a "bocadillo" (sandwich) or a pastry from a local bakery for an energy boost and a taste of the local lifestyle.

Remember, the best food experiences come from venturing beyond the tourist path. So, embrace your inner foodie explorer, delve into local markets and restaurants, and discover the true flavors of Valencia – all without spending a fortune!

Transportation Tips

Valencia boasts a vibrant and efficient public transport network, making getting around the city a breeze. But for the budget-conscious traveler and the adventurous soul, alternative modes like cycling offer a unique perspective and a chance to experience the city at your own pace. Here's your guide to conquering both:

Public Transport Prowess

- **T-Valencia Card:** Your key to unlocking the city's public transport system. Purchase this rechargeable card for unlimited rides on buses,

trams, and the metro, making sightseeing affordable and convenient.
• **Buses & Trams:** Explore the city's diverse neighborhoods with an extensive network of buses and trams. Download the EMT Valencia app for real-time schedules and route planning.
• **Metro Magic:** Beat the traffic and quickly reach major attractions with the efficient metro system. The network covers key areas, making it a great option for longer journeys.

Cycling Your Way Through Valencia:
• **Rent a Bike:** Several companies offer bike rentals at reasonable prices. Explore the city at your own pace, stopping at hidden gems and enjoying the fresh air.
• **Bike Lanes & Green Spaces:** Valencia prioritizes cyclists with dedicated lanes and green spaces like the Turia Gardens, perfect for a scenic ride.
• **Safety First:** Always wear a helmet and obey traffic regulations for a safe and enjoyable cycling experience.

Beyond the Obvious:
• **Valencia Bikeshare:** For short trips, consider the Valenbisi bikeshare program. Pick up a bike at

designated stations and return it to another for a small fee.
- **Boat Tours:** Take a unique perspective of the city with a boat tour along the Turia River or the canals of the Albufera Natural Park.
- **Walking:** Lace up your walking shoes and explore the charming old town at your own pace, discovering hidden squares and local shops.

Remember:

- **Validate tickets:** Always validate your public transport tickets upon boarding to avoid fines.
- **Buy tickets in advance:** Purchase T-Valencia cards or multi-day passes for convenience and potential discounts.
- **Respect fellow travelers:** Be mindful of others on public transport and on the road while cycling.
- **Embrace the unexpected:** Get lost, explore hidden corners, and let Valencia surprise you with its diverse transport options.

By utilizing public transport efficiently and considering alternative modes like cycling, you can navigate Valencia like a local, save money, and experience the city in a whole new light. So, grab your T-Valencia card, hop on a bike, and get ready to explore!

CHAPTER 8: ITINERARY

3 Days

Valencia beckons with its rich history, futuristic architecture, and stunning beaches. Embrace the city's diverse personality with this 3-day itinerary, packed with exciting experiences and hidden gems.

Day 1: Immerse Yourself in History
• **Morning:** Start your day with a journey through time at the Valencia Cathedral. Climb the Miguelete bell tower for panoramic views (2€ entry), then explore the intricate details inside. Next, head to the La Lonja de la Seda (free entry), a UNESCO World Heritage Site that whispers tales of Valencia's silk trade.
• **Afternoon:** Immerse yourself in the city's vibrant past at the Valencia History Museum (2€ entry). Interactive exhibits bring history to life, from Roman ruins to medieval battles. Afterwards, wander through the charming El Carmen neighborhood, admiring its historical architecture and hidden plazas.
• **Evening:** Enjoy a traditional paella dinner in a local restaurant in Ruzafa, followed by a lively flamenco show in one of the city's tablaos.

Day 2: Embrace the Future

• **Morning:** Step into a sci-fi movie set at the Ciudad de las Artes y las Ciencias. Explore the Hemisfèric's giant IMAX cinema (9€ entry) or get lost in the interactive exhibits of the Science Museum (8€ entry). Don't miss the stunning nighttime illuminations that transform the buildings into glowing giants.

• **Afternoon:** Dive into the underwater world at the L'Oceanogràfic aquarium (31€ entry). Witness the diverse marine life, from playful penguins to majestic sharks, in underwater tunnels and dazzling exhibitions. Afterwards, relax on the nearby Malvarrosa Beach, taking a dip in the crystal-clear Mediterranean waters.

• **Evening:** Take a stroll along the Turia Gardens, a sprawling urban oasis transformed from a former riverbed. Enjoy a picnic under the palm trees or rent a bike for a scenic ride. In the evening, head to the lively Cabanyal neighborhood for delicious tapas and a vibrant atmosphere.

Day 3: Explore Nature and Local Gems

• **Morning:** Escape the city bustle and explore the Albufera Natural Park. Take a boat tour through the rice paddies and lagoons (8€ entry with boat tour),

spotting diverse birdlife and soaking in the tranquil atmosphere.
- **Afternoon:** Visit the Central Market, a feast for the senses overflowing with fresh produce, local delicacies, and handcrafted goods. Sample seasonal fruits and cured meats or grab a delicious "bocadillo" (sandwich) for a picnic.
- **Evening:** End your trip with a cultural experience. Visit the Valencia Institute of Modern Art (IVAM) for contemporary art exhibitions (free entry on Sundays), or attend a concert at the Palau de la Música (ticket prices vary). Alternatively, enjoy a farewell dinner at a restaurant with breathtaking views from the Torres de Quart (5€ entry).

Bonus:

If you're visiting in March, witness the Fallas Festival, a UNESCO-recognized celebration featuring giant satirical monuments and spectacular pyrotechnics.

In July, immerse yourself in the Feria de Julio, offering music, dance, bullfighting, and traditional Valencian culture.

7 days Itinerary

Valencia's vibrant personality unfolds as you delve deeper. This 7-day itinerary offers a balanced mix of history, science, nature, and local experiences, ensuring you savor the city's soul:

Day 1: Historical Heartbeat
• **Morning:** Start your journey at the iconic Valencia Cathedral (2€ entry). Climb the Miguelete bell tower for breathtaking panoramas, imagining the city's evolution. Immerse yourself in the La Lonja de la Seda (free entry), a UNESCO gem whispering tales of the city's silk trade.
• **Afternoon:** Delve into history at the Valencia History Museum (2€ entry), with interactive exhibits bringing Roman ruins and medieval battles to life. Wander charming El Carmen, admiring its historical architecture and hidden plazas.
• **Evening:** Savor a traditional paella dinner in Ruzafa, followed by a passionate flamenco show in a local "tablao."

Day 2: Artistic Expressions
• **Morning:** Explore the IVAM (free entry on Sundays), Valencia's Institute of Modern Art, showcasing contemporary masterpieces.

- **Afternoon:** Witness the avant-garde architecture of the Ciudad de las Artes y las Ciencias. Journey through the Hemisfèric's IMAX cinema (9€ entry) or unravel scientific wonders at the Science Museum (8€ entry). Don't miss the enchanting nighttime illuminations.

Day 3: Culinary Delights & Relaxation
- **Morning:** Indulge in the sensory overload of the Central Market. Sample seasonal fruits and local delicacies, or grab a "bocadillo" for a picnic.
- **Afternoon:** Escape the city's buzz with a boat tour through the Albufera Natural Park (8€ entry with boat tour). Witness breathtaking landscapes, diverse birdlife, and the tranquility of the rice paddies.
- **Evening:** Rejuvenate on Malvarrosa Beach, basking in the sun and taking a refreshing dip in the Mediterranean. Savor local tapas and vibrant atmosphere in the Cabanyal neighborhood.

Day 4: Beyond the Tourist Trail
- **Morning:** Cycle through the scenic Turia Gardens, a former riverbed transformed into a green oasis. Visit the Ceramic Museum (3€ entry), showcasing Valencia's rich ceramic heritage.

- **Afternoon:** Travel back in time at the Serranos Towers (2€ entry), offering panoramic views and a glimpse into Valencia's medieval past.
- **Evening:** Enjoy a traditional dinner at a restaurant in Ruzafa, followed by a live music performance in a local bar.

Day 5: Nature's Embrace

- **Morning:** Take a day trip to the charming town of Jativa, birthplace of the Borgia family. Explore the imposing hilltop castle and the majestic collegiate church.
- **Afternoon:** Immerse yourself in the natural beauty of the Chulilla Gorge, a haven for hiking, swimming, and stunning scenery.

Day 6: Festival Fiesta!

Immerse yourself in the city's vibrant spirit during Fallas Festival (March) with its giant satirical monuments and breathtaking pyrotechnics.

Alternatively, experience the lively Feria de Julio (July) with its traditional music, dance, bullfighting, and cultural events.

Day 7: Farewell Flavors

- **Morning:** Visit the vibrant Ruzafa Market for souvenirs and local treats. Browse unique handicrafts and savor freshly baked goods.

- **Afternoon:** Bid farewell to Valencia with a delightful lunch at a restaurant overlooking the Torres de Quart (5€ entry) for a final dose of history and panoramic views.

Bonus:
- Catch a sunset boat tour along the Turia River for a romantic and unique perspective of the city.
- Take a Spanish language class to connect with locals and enhance your cultural experience.
- Attend a traditional Valencian cooking class to learn the secrets of local cuisine and recreate the flavors at home.

Remember:
- This itinerary is flexible, adapt it to your interests and preferences.

Consider purchasing the Valencia • Tourist Card for discounts and public transportation access.
- Embrace the "siesta" culture and enjoy leisurely lunches and relaxed evenings.

Strike up conversations with locals – they're often happy to share hidden gems and insider tips.

2 Weeks Itinerary

With two weeks in Valencia, you have the luxury to go deeper into its vibrant personality, venture beyond the city limits, and truly immerse yourself in the local rhythm. Here's an itinerary that blends historical exploration, artistic discoveries, nature escapes, and cultural experiences:

Week 1:
- **Days 1-3:** Follow the Days 1-3 itinerary from the 7-day version, immersing yourself in the city's historical heart, artistic expressions, and culinary delights.
- **Day 4:** Explore the Serranos Towers and the Ceramic Museum as suggested in the 7-day itinerary. In the afternoon, embark on a historical walking tour led by a local guide, delving into hidden corners, forgotten stories, and lesser-known landmarks.
- **Day 5:** Take a day trip to Sagunto, a charming coastal town with a rich Roman and medieval heritage. Explore the imposing hilltop castle, the Roman theater, and the charming old town.
- **Day 6:** Enjoy a leisurely morning at the Central Market, savoring the sights and smells of fresh produce and local delicacies. In the afternoon, relax

on Malvarrosa Beach, participating in water sports like paddle boarding or kayaking.
- **Days 7-8:** Escape the city's bustle by exploring the Sierra Calderona Natural Park. Hike through scenic trails, discover hidden waterfalls, and enjoy breathtaking mountain views. Stay overnight in a charming village nestled within the park.

Week 2

- **Days 9-10:** Immerse yourself in the Fallas Festival (March) or the Feria de Julio (July), experiencing the vibrant spirit of these traditional celebrations. Alternatively, visit the nearby city of Alicante for its majestic Santa Bárbara castle and lively atmosphere.
- **Day 11:** Explore the diverse marine life at the L'Oceanogràfic aquarium, followed by a relaxing afternoon at the Malvarrosa Beach. In the evening, enjoy a flamenco show and a delicious tapas dinner in the El Carmen neighborhood.
- **Days 12-13:** Take a day trip to the Albufera Natural Park, a haven for birdwatchers and nature enthusiasts. Enjoy a boat tour through the rice paddies, visit the traditional fishing village of El Palmar, and savor a paella lunch made with fresh local seafood.
- **Day 14:** Visit the IVAM for a dose of contemporary art, followed by a leisurely stroll

through the Turia Gardens. In the evening, attend a concert at the Palau de la Música, immersing yourself in Valencia's rich cultural scene.

CONCLUSION

Valencia, like a kaleidoscope in your palm, has spun its magic, its vibrant fragments now glittering in your memory. You've traced the echoes of history on ancient streets, stood awestruck beneath architectural jewels, and savored flavors that danced on your tongue. Perhaps you chased futuristic visions within the City of Arts and Sciences, or felt history whisper secrets in the Silk Exchange. Maybe you soaked in the tranquility of the Albufera, or chased laughter alongside waves on Malvarrosa Beach.

Remember, Valencia's essence lingers long after your departure. It's the warmth of the sun on your skin, the joy of shared laughter in a lively tapas bar, the rhythm of flamenco forever etched in your heart. It's the serendipitous encounters, the hidden treasures unearthed, and the stories whispered by weathered walls.

As you embark on your next adventure, carry a piece of Valencia within you. Let it be the spirit of exploration that fueled your journey, the newfound appreciation for diverse cultures, or simply the lingering taste of a perfect paella, a reminder of sun-drenched days. Share your Valencian tales, inspiring others to weave their own stories into the city's vibrant tapestry.

But Valencia is more than a destination; it's an open invitation. It's a promise whispered on the wind, a city that awaits your return, ready to unveil new secrets and add another layer to your unique memories. So, hasta luego, Valencia. Until we meet again, bajo el sol español (under the Spanish sun).

Perhaps, let's replace the closing sentence with a more personal sentiment based on your specific experiences. Did you fall in love with a certain neighborhood? Discover a hidden gem you want to share? Mention it in the review section to leave a truly lasting impression and inspire other readers to create their own unforgettable Valencian adventure.